MID TO LATER INTERMEDIATE

CHRISTMAS TIME

Arranged by Carolyn C. Setliff

ISBN 1-4234-1438-1

WILLIS MUSIC

EXCLUSIVELY DISTRIBUTED BY

HAL•LEONARD®
CORPORATION
7777 W. BLUEMOUND RD. P.O. BOX 13819 MILWAUKEE, WI 53213

In Australia Contact:
Hal Leonard Australia Pty. Ltd.
4 Lentara Court
Cheltenham, Victoria, 3192 Australia
Email: ausadmin@halleonard.com

Visit Hal Leonard Online at
www.halleonard.com

FOREWORD

I love Christmas! These arrangements were especially written for use in recitals, church services and special programs, as well as for personal enjoyment with family and friends. My hope is that each one who plays and hears these Christmas arrangements will be filled anew with the love, hope and joy that Christmas brings.

Carolyn C. Setliff

Carol of the Bells

Ukrainian Christmas Carol
Arranged by Carolyn C. Setliff

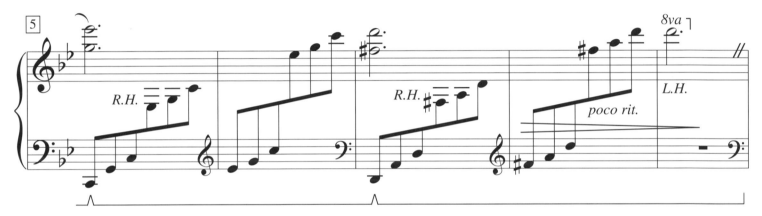

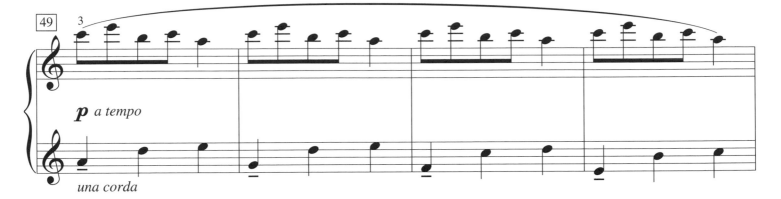

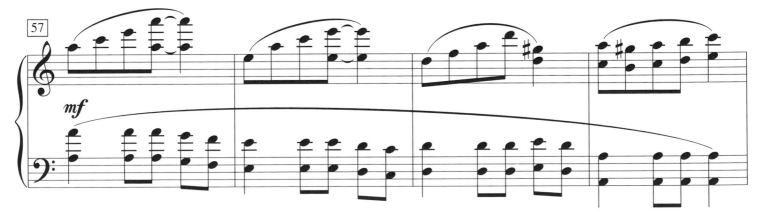

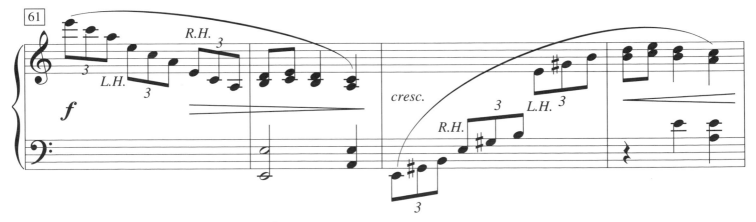

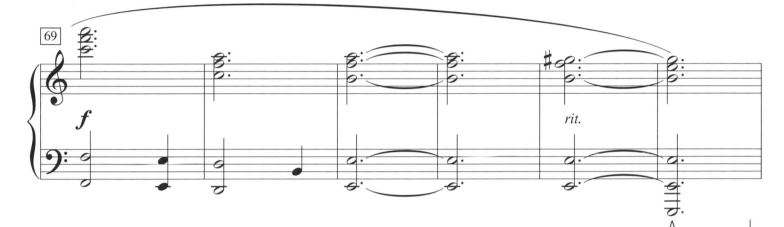

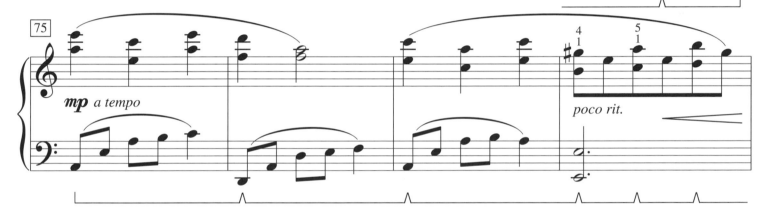

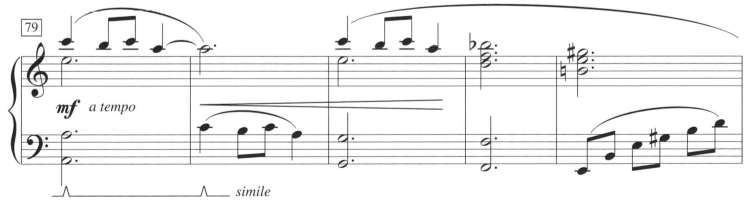

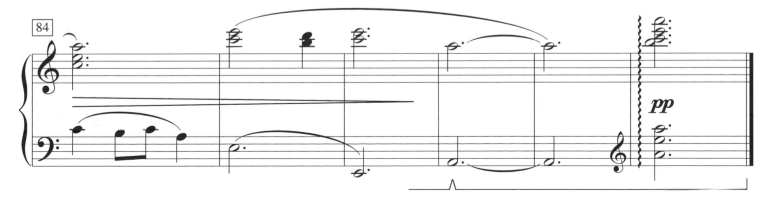

Sing We Now of Christmas

Traditional
Arranged by Carolyn C. Setliff

with pedal to end

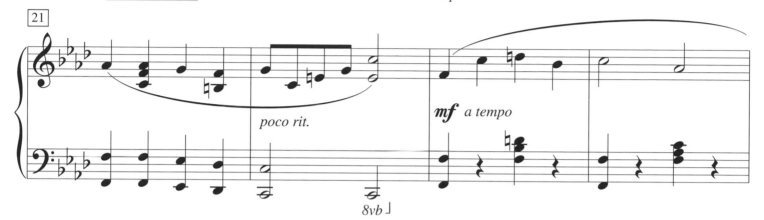

poco rit.

mf *a tempo*

8vb

Flowing, with rubato

poco rit.

mf *a tempo*

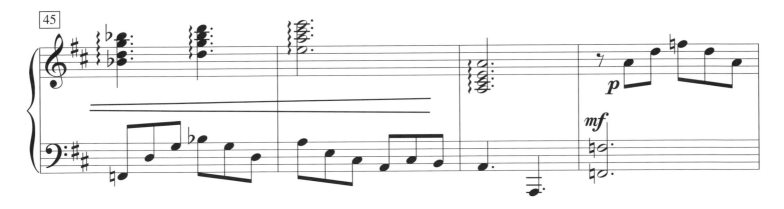

Majestic, slower tempo

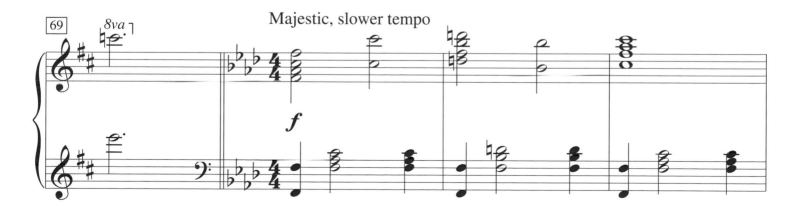

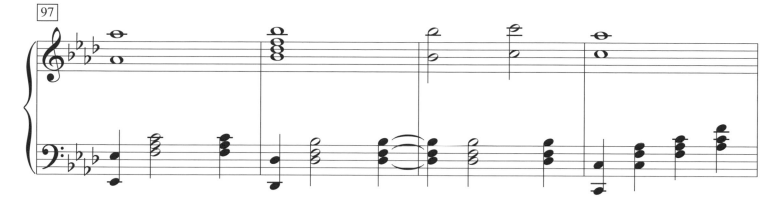

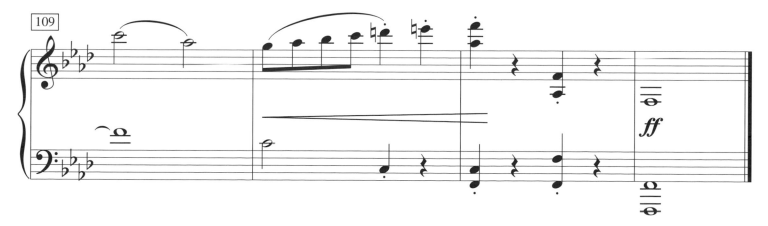

The First Noel

17th Century English Carol
Music from W. Sandys' *Christmas Carols*
Arranged by Carolyn C. Setliff

Tenderly

mp

With pedal

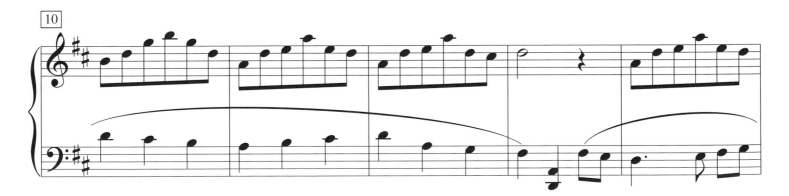

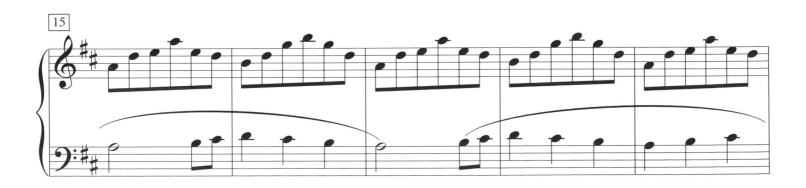

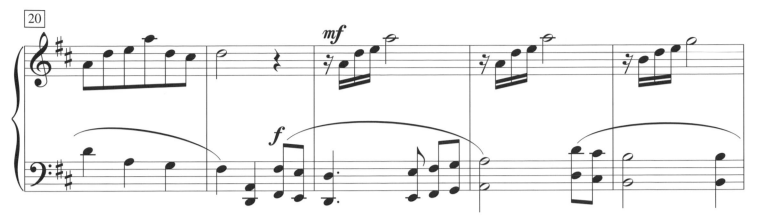

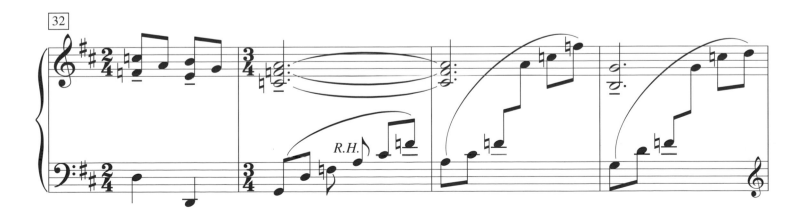

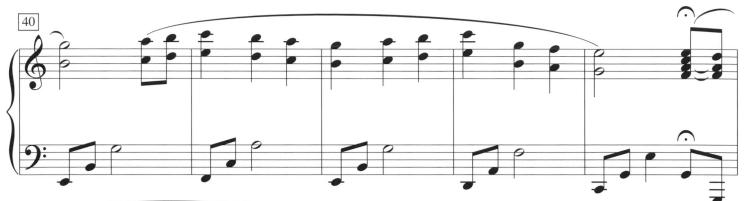

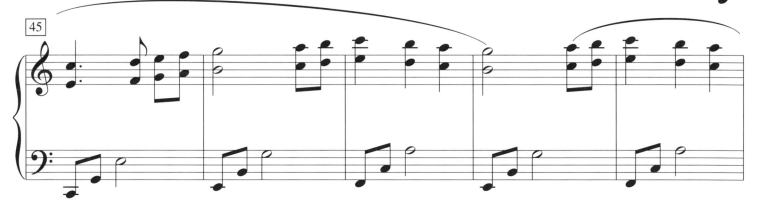

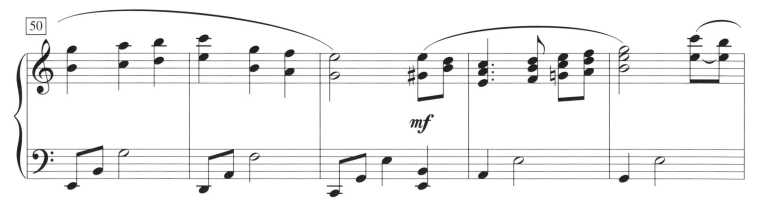

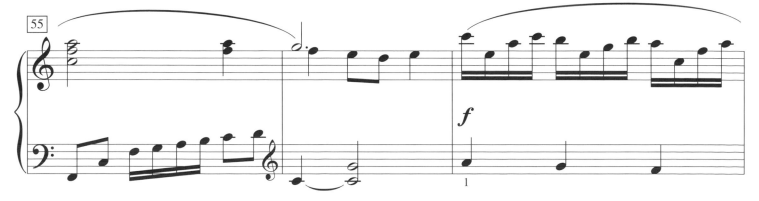

The Snow Lay on the Ground

Traditional Irish Carol
Arranged by Carolyn C. Setliff

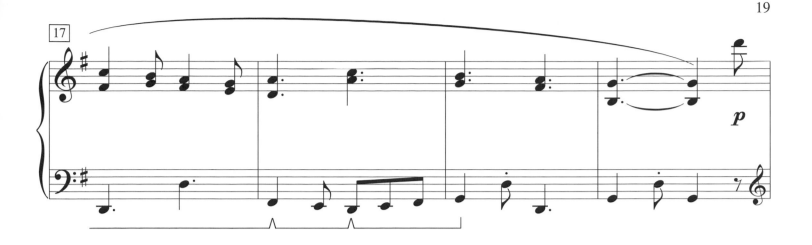

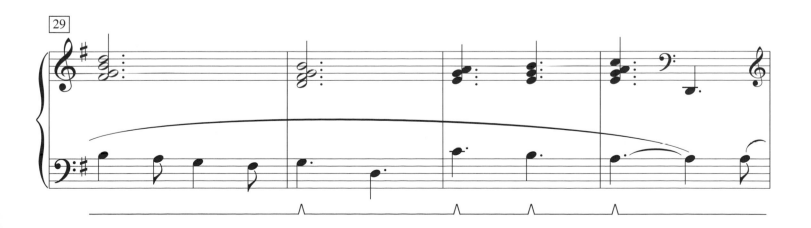

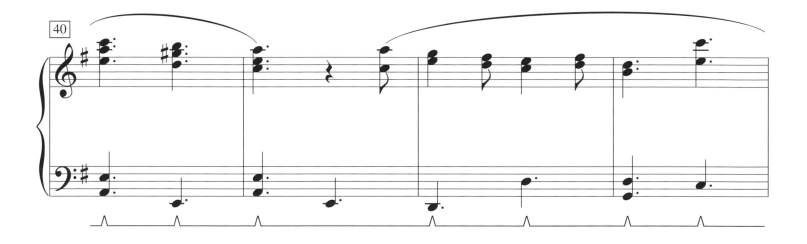

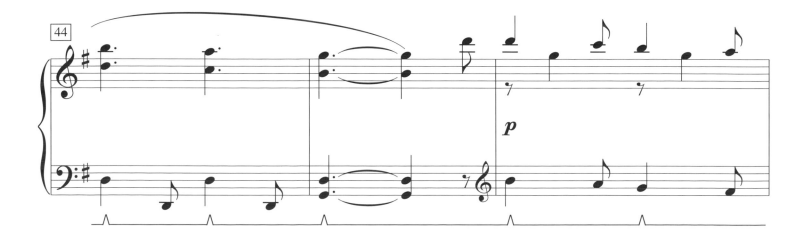

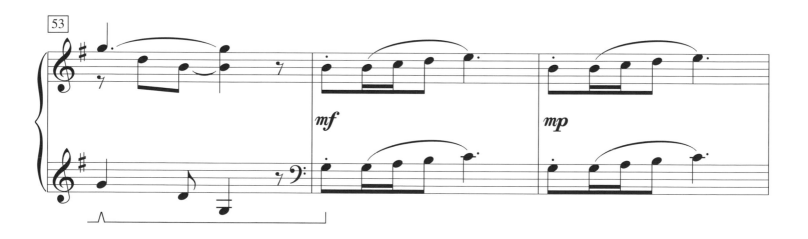

In the Bleak Midwinter

Poem by Christina Rossetti
Music by Gustav Holst
Arranged by Carolyn C. Setliff

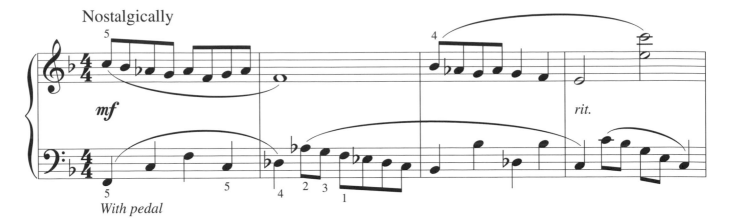

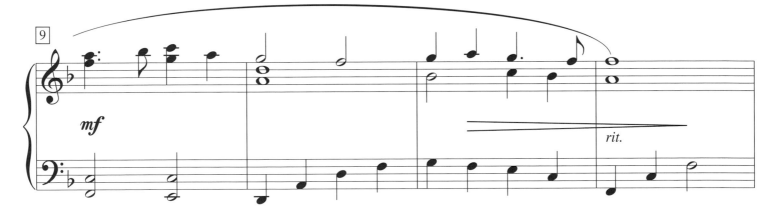

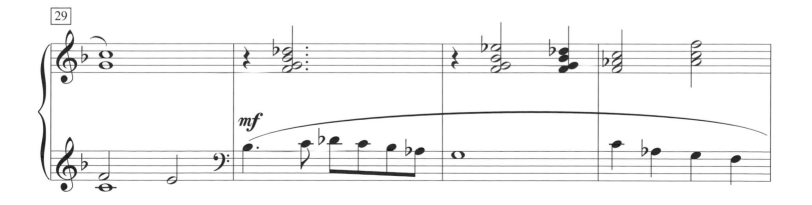

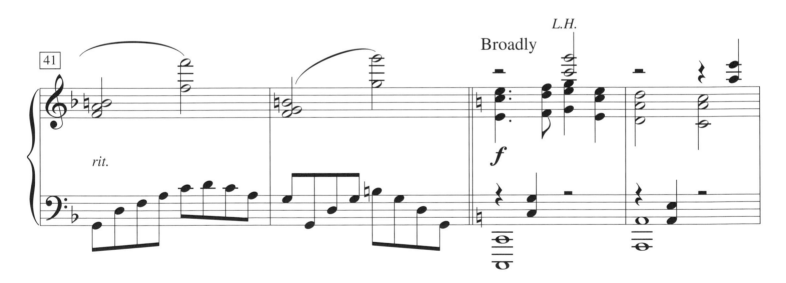

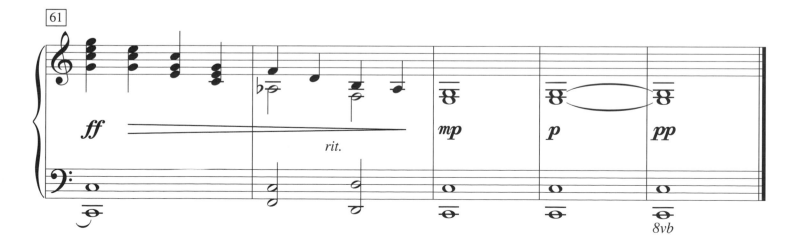

O Holy Night

French words by Placide Cappeau
English words by John S. Dwight
Music by Adolphe Adam
Arranged by Carolyn C. Setliff

Ding Dong! Merrily on High!

French Carol
Arranged by Carolyn C. Setliff

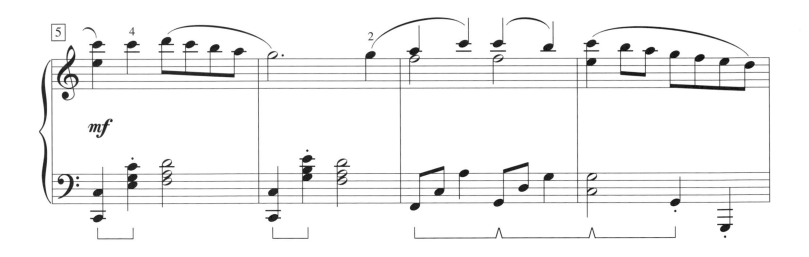

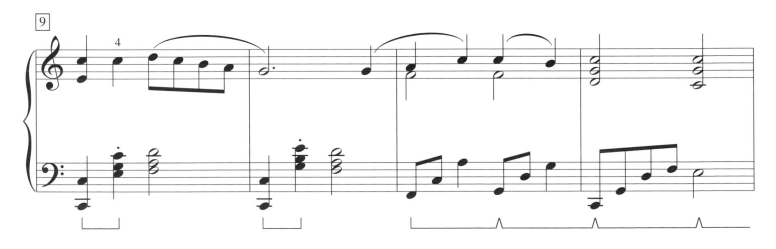

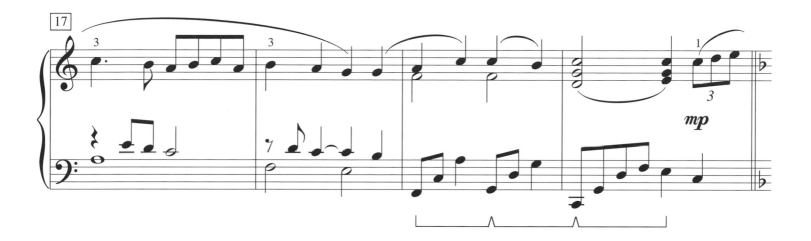

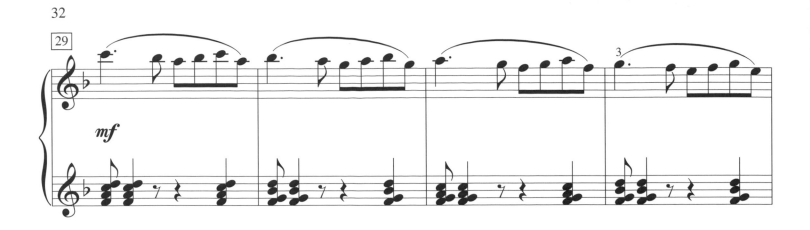

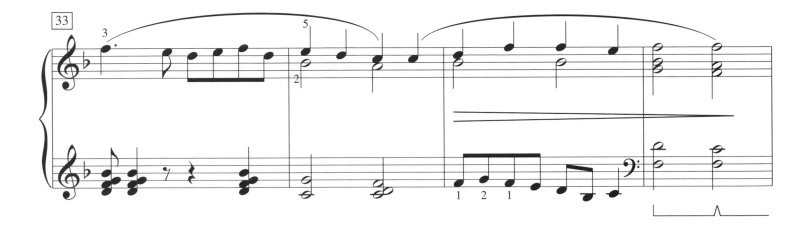